GAMES TO PLAY WITH BABIES

By "Miss Jackie" Weissman

Thank You

to our many contributors—
moms, dads and grandparents

Mary Ann Herron	Erin Vancil	Jack Marshall
Elaine Fowler	Peggy Hulstine	Gene Hulstine
Ania Johnson	Ruth Marshall	Gloria McDaniel
Elizabeth Stucki	Bertha Silberg	Meryl Miller
Margaret Hake	Susan Labunski	Jerry Maloney

© 1988 by Jackie Weissman

ISBN 0 - 939514 - 10 - 9

Third Printing

Published by MISS JACKIE MUSIC COMPANY,
10001 El Monte, Overland Park, Kansas 66207.

Printed in the United States of America.

Cover design by Cynthia Fowler.

Illustrations by Ania Johnson and Susan Labunski.

Distributed by
Gryphon House
3706 Otis Street
PO Box 211
Mt. Rainier, Maryland 20822

From the Author

This book has written itself over the past several years. It is an outgrowth of the classes that I teach for parents and babies together.

When we meet to share music, movement, games, fun, loving and bonding, the parents have shared many games that they play with their babies.

All the games in this book have been played and enjoyed. They come from a variety of cultures and ethnic backgrounds. They have also been played with "special" children. The people who submitted the games are parents, grandparents, aunts, uncles, cousins, etc.

★ Note: The age groups for the games in this book were submitted by the contributors and are intended only as a general guide. Your baby may do the activities earlier or later than the age group indicated.

Positive bonding and attachment to a loving caregiver give a baby emotional security that aids in his/her total development.

These games will give you and your baby much pleasure. They will improve baby's listening and language skills, motor development, cognitive skills and sense of humor, and give you both a loving, bonding experience.

Play these games with your baby. Hold your baby close and cuddle, pat, touch, kiss and enjoy!

—Jackie Weissman

Miss Jackie

Table of Contents

Growing and Learning Games

Kitchen Games

Laughing and Having Fun Games

Bath and Dressing Games

Guidelines for Growth

Growing
and
Learning
Games

Rattles and Teethers

Purpose: To experience the pleasure of mouthing

Play this game when the baby is alert. A crib or infant seat is a good place to play the game.

Put a rattle in the baby's hand. (It doesn't matter if it's the left or right hand—eventually, the baby will make that choice.) The baby may hold the rattle for only a few seconds, then drop it. Pick it up and give it to the baby again.

Soon, the baby will bring the rattle to his/her mouth. At this stage of development, objects in a baby's hand become something for the mouth. When it's time to add a teether, you will know.

All Around the House

Purpose: Teaching opposites

Hold the baby and move about the house talking and demonstrating the following things.

The light is off—the light is on.

The door is open—the door is closed.

The towel is on the rack—the towel is on the floor.

I'm lifting you up—I'm lifting you down.

The cup is full—the cup is empty (in the bathtub).

Doing the actions for the baby until the baby can do them for him/her will motivate the child tremendously.

How Does It Feel?

Purpose: Discovering texture

Take a small, thin box and punch two fingerholes in it. Line the box with different textures—fur, burlap, velvet, sandpaper.

Show the baby how to poke a finger in the hole. You can poke your finger in the other hole. Talk to the baby about how it feels—soft, rough, bumpy, etc.

This game is nice to take in the car.

Shake, Shake, Shake

Purpose: Sound discrimination

Fill several small plastic containers with different objects—bells, dry beans, rice, marbles, etc. Film canisters and plastic eggs are good containers. Be sure you have the lids on tightly so that the baby cannot remove the contents.

Give a container to the baby and, holding the baby's hand, shake the container. Say the words "Shake, shake" as you do this. Then, give the baby another container and do the same thing.

This is a beginning game in sound discrimination, which in turn develops language.

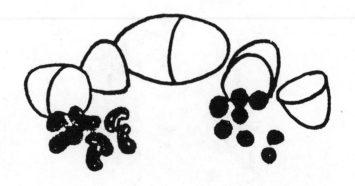

Left, Right, Cross the Street

Purpose: Pre-reading and safety

When crossing the street with your baby, instead of saying "Let's look both ways before crossing," change your words and turn it into a game.

Say to your baby, "Now we are at the corner. We are going to cross the street. But first, let's make sure that no cars are coming. Look to the left *(turn the stroller or the child to face left)*. No cars? Okay, now let's look to the right *(turn the stroller or the child to face right)*. No cars? Good. It's okay to cross." *(Then cross the street.)*

With a toddler, play the same game holding hands.

The child learns traffic safety while learning to distinguish left from right.

Touch This

Purpose: Tactile discrimination

Find a quiet time when you and your baby can play together uninterrupted. Gather together items that have different kinds of "feel" to them. For example: foil, cotton balls, emery boards, corduroy, velvet, satin, wool, waxed paper, cork.

Glue different-textured objects on a large piece of cardboard. Put your baby's hand on each one and tell the baby what he/she is touching as you do it. Make comments like "smooth," "nice," "soft" and "cool."

This is also excellent for language development.

Look! I Can Pour!

Purpose: Fine motor development

Sit on the floor with your baby with some paper cups and dry cereal (Cheerios works well) in front of you.

Fill a cup with the cereal and show the baby how to pour the cereal from one cup to another. Then, let the baby try pouring.

Little ones will spend much time doing this activity until they get it right. They also enjoy eating what spills.

The next step in pouring development is to work with water. Do this in an area that you won't mind the spills. The bathtub is a perfect place.

Drop the Clothespin

Purpose: Fine motor skills

The object of the game is to drop clothespins into a container. Use a coffee can or gallon milk container with the opening made larger than the clothespins.

Show the baby how to hold the clothespin so that it will drop into the opening. You will have to tilt the container at first to help the child be successful.

Show the child how to turn the container upside down to remove the clothespins.

Roll It Back

Purpose: Small motor development

You will need a soft fabric ball. Sit on the floor facing the baby and roll the ball to the baby. Take the baby's hands and show him/her how to roll it back to you.

This is great fun for the baby and, with a little encouragement, he/she will learn very quickly to roll the ball back.

When babies start throwing things out of the crib, this is a sign that they are ready to play this game.

Moving Around the House

Purpose: Vocabulary and listening skills

Play this game using a doll house plus toys and/or dolls. Instruct the child to put a toy or doll in various rooms. "Go to the kitchen." "Go to the living room."

This activity can also be played using a series of magazine pictures of various rooms or a clearly identified floor plan.

Stand in the center of your own house. Tell the child to go to a certain room and hide. You will try to find him/her.

Where Did It Go?

*Purpose: Cognitive—an objects still exists, even if it's
out of sight*

Face the baby and show him/her a favorite toy. Let the
baby play with it for a few minutes, then ask the baby
if you can have a turn. If the baby agrees, take the toy
and cover it with a cloth that is easily within the baby's
grasp.

Help the baby find the toy, then repeat the game. You
might want to ask "Where is the toy?" or something
similar. Make a kind of mystery out of it.

Play the game several times until the baby knows
where the toy is and can find it. Next, do the same
game with a different toy or object.

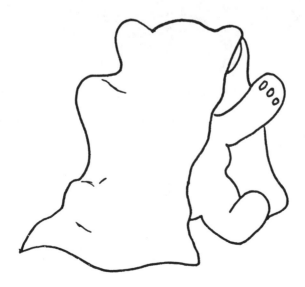

Raindrops on My Face

Purpose: Experiencing nature

Take your baby outside and discover all kinds of wonderful things. Feel the wind in your hair, raindrops on your face, smell a flower, watch a butterfly, wiggle worms in your hand. Lie in the grass and look at the clouds, squish your toes in mud. The possibilities are endless!

Some more things to do: crunch an autumn leaf, jump in a pile of leaves. Care for plants and watch them grow; taste fresh fruits and vegetables from the garden (strawberries, tomatoes). Taste a snowflake.

Clip the Clothespin

Purpose: Fine motor development

Get a large canister that has smooth edges when the lid is removed. (A popcorn canister is excellent for this.) Take a clothespin and show your baby how to slip the clothespin onto the can.

Babies seem to be fascinated with this and it is excellent for fine motor coordination and eye-hand coordination.

Give the baby several clothespins for putting on the can, then show how the clothespins can be dropped into the can.

Two games with the same objects.

Building Blocks

Purpose: Fine motor coordination

Sit down on the floor with your baby. Put one block on the floor and say, "I am putting one block on the floor." Add a block and say, "I am putting two blocks on the floor." Do the same thing with three blocks. Then, knock down the tower and let the baby build it up—with your help, if necessary.

As your child's coordination increases, the tower will get taller. You can also ask the child to tell you how many blocks are in the tower. Talk about the color of the blocks, too.

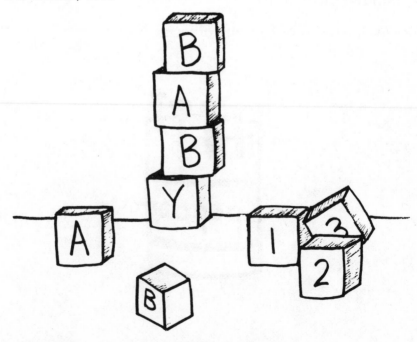

Hello . . . Who's There?

Purpose: Language development

Get a pretend telephone, so that when you are through your baby can pretend, too.

Say "Ding-a-ling, ding-a-ling." Pretend the phone is ringing and answer it. As you are talking to the pretend person (someone the baby knows, like grandparents, a friend, etc.), also talk to the baby. For example, "Hello, Grandpa." Then say to the baby, "It's your grandpa." Talk about a special activity, a visit, a meal or maybe plans for the day—something the baby is familiar with and will understand.

Be sure to say "Good-bye" and hang up the phone. Then, give the phone to your baby and let him/her have a pretend conversation.

What's in the Drawer?

Purpose: Exploring the world

Curiosity is the backbone of the development of competence. As your child's very earliest perceptions grow, he/she will want to feel and explore everything, to experience the world through all five senses.

In a small, easily opened drawer in the kitchen, place many different objects: plastic containers, pans, wooden spoons, anything that doesn't have sharp edges and is safe for children to play with. Leave the drawer ajar while you are in the kitchen and you will have a happy, curious companion who is bent on exploring this drawer. From time to time, change what is in the drawer.

Bean Bag Fun

Purpose: Developing the creative process

Bean bags are an excellent toy for young children.
They are safe, soft and stimulate creativity.

Think of all the things you can do with bean bags while
playing with your baby: throw them, stack them, put
them on your head, put them on your back, put them
on your tummy, lie on your back with your feet in the
air and balance a bean bag on each foot, drop them
into things, etc.

Make-Believe House

Purpose: Developing creativity

Make a tent or playhouse for your child. (A simple tent can be made by putting a sheet over the backs of two to four chairs or over a card table.)

If you want more detail, you can make walls and a roof out of felt for the card table. You could also decorate the walls.

You can pretend that your tent is a cave, an airplane, a train, a spaceship or a house. You can take a pillow, blanket and stuffed toy inside your pretend house.

Blocks Can Be Anything

Purpose: Imaginative play

Help your child learn to pretend with blocks. Take a block in your hand and move it along the floor. Tell the child, "Here is Susie, driving in the car." Make up other phrases to go with your block story, such as "Beep-beep, look out, you cars!" or "Time to stop for the light."

Help encourage the child to turn the blocks into other imaginative ideas. Pretend the blocks are two different people carrying on a conversation.

This kind of activity encourages creative development.

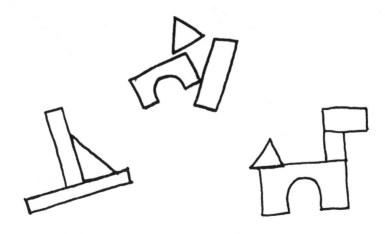

Can You Do This?

Purpose: Enjoying baby's reflection in a mirror

Hold the baby in your arms and stand in front of a large mirror. Say to the baby, "Look, see the pretty baby?"

Make animated facial expressions in the mirror while the baby watches. Your baby will imitate your actions.

Hold up the baby's arm and say, "See the baby's arm?" Do this with different body parts.

Kiss the baby. Kiss your reflection. Blink your eyes. Play peek-a-boo.

This is a great game for a fussy baby.

Magic Mud

Purpose: Observing changes

Mix a box of cornstarch and enough water to form the consistency of bread dough. If you roll the mixture, it will form a ball. If you let it rest, it will return to liquid.

Sing the following song as you roll the cornstarch.

To the tune of "Row, Row, Row Your Boat."

*Take some magic mud
And roll it in a ball.
Now we will sit so still
And watch it disappear.*

Say to the baby, "Let's be very quiet and watch the magic."

29

Watch the Birds Eat

Purpose: Observation and bonding

Birds are fascinating to watch, and it makes a very enjoyable activity to do with your baby.

Make a simple bird feeder using a pinecone. Spread it with peanut butter and then roll it in birdseed. Hang it near a window where it can be observed easily.

Talk with your baby about what the birds eat, where they find food, etc.

You will be amazed at the different birds that will show up at your feeder. It's a chance to talk about the color, size, language of birds and much more.

In the Bag

Purpose: Cognitive skills

Get a large shopping bag or a grocery sack. Ask your child to bring you specific items to put into the sack.

Ask for one object at a time, letting your child put each thing into the sack. Always say "Thank you" each time the child brings the item.

Some suggestions are a favorite toy, silverware, a blanket or towel, a toothbrush, etc. Select things that your child can reach and bring to you on his/her own.

This game develops the thinking process. The child hears the word, makes an association and then finds the object. A wonderful mind-developing game.

Do What I Do

Purpose: Cognitive growth

Play a game of imitation with your baby. Do actions and let the child imitate you: wave your hands, wiggle your fingers, stomp your feet, pretend to be asleep, etc.

Now, let the child do something while *you* imitate him/her. You may have to give a suggestion, at first, for what the child should do.

Adapt this activity to jobs around the house and the yard—raking leaves, dusting, sweeping, etc.

Whee! Over the Book!

Purpose: Developing gross motor skills

Put a small book on the floor. Show the child how to jump over the book. Sing to the tune of "Here We Go 'Round the Mulberry Bush."

I am jumping over the book,
Over the book, over the book.
I am jumping over the book.
See me jumping now. . . . WHEE!

Now, hold the child's arms and sing the song again. On the words "See me jumping now. . . . WHEE!" lift the child up and jump him/her over the book. Replace the word "me" with the child's name.

Repeat again and again. When the child can do it alone, add a new object for jumping. The second object for jumping could be a little larger than the first.

You can also do other actions over the book: hopping, flying, swimming, going backward, etc.

Opening Jars

Purpose: Developing fine motor skills

Gather together some plastic jars with lids small enough for little hands to hold. Put a favorite toy in the jar and close the lid. Let your child open the jar to retrieve the toy.

Your child will want to practice this game over and over.

Hippity Hoppity

Purpose: Counting

Say the poem and do the actions.

Hippity hoppity hippity hay,
Five little bunnies went out to play.
  (Five fingers hopping)
Hippity hoppity hippity hay,
One little bunny hopped away.
  (Hand behind back)
Hippity hoppity hippity hay,
Four little bunnies went out to play.
  (Four fingers hopping)

Repeat and bring back three fingers, etc.

Hippity hoppity hippity ho
Where did all the bunnies go?
  (Bring back all five bunnies)

Talk about where the bunnies might have gone—to take a nap, to search for food, etc.

Kitchen
Games

Mouth Noises

Purpose: Pre-language development

Imitate the mouth noises your baby makes. Also, encourage your baby to imitate your noises. Try the following with your baby.

★ Kissing

★ Tongue clicking

★ A raspberry

★ Sucking your front teeth with your tongue

★ Making a "ch-ch" sound

★ Sticking an index finger in your mouth and then popping the finger out

★ Blowing out and sucking in air

★ Making a "bub-bub" sound by moving your lips back and forth with your index finger while humming

What's Cooking?

Purpose: Language development

Sit your baby safely in the kitchen, in an infant seat or swing. As you are preparing a meal, talk about each thing that you are doing.

"I'm stirring."

"I'm pouring."

"I'm measuring."

Let the baby play with measuring spoons, bowls, wooden spoons, etc. When the baby is old enough, begin to let him/her help pour, beat and stir.

Always name each ingredient as you use it.

Bang It and Shake It

Purpose: Motor development

This game is good to play during an alert time for the baby. Sit the baby in a high chair or on an uncarpeted floor.

Attract the baby's attention by banging a block on the table or floor. Encourage your child to do the same and express your delight at his/her attempt.

Repeat this activity by shaking a rattle.

When the baby gets the idea of holding on and shaking or banging, it's nice to sing a song as you shake or bang. Any nursery rhyme like "Mary Had a Little Lamb" or "Farmer in the Dell" works very well.

39

Three Blocks, Two Hands

Purpose: Learning to release objects

Put your baby in a high chair or on the floor. Place two blocks on the floor in front of the baby. If the baby doesn't pick up a block, put it in his/her hand.

Now, take a third block and give it to the baby. He/she will learn to drop one block in order to pick up another.

Smells So Good

Purpose: Developing a sense of smell

Play this game in the kitchen when the baby is alert.
Put the baby in a safe place where he/she can watch
what you're doing.

Gather together flavorings and spices that you have in
your kitchen. Let the baby smell the different flavorings
and spices. You will be surprised at how the baby will
respond to this immediately.

Whenever a situation presents itself, encourage the
baby to smell—flowers, grass, shampoo, fruit at the
supermarket, etc. Remember to always tell the baby
what he/she is smelling.

This is a very important game for olfactory
discrimination.

I Can Do It Myself

Purpose: Develop fine motor skills

Have small pieces of round oat cereal or small pieces of banana on hand. Put a piece of cereal on the baby's high chair. Pick it up and put it in your mouth. As you do this, say "I pick up the cereal and put it in my mouth. Yum, yum, yum."

Now, take the baby's hand and help the baby pick up the cereal, saying, "*(Child's name)* picks up the cereal and puts it in his/her mouth. Yum, yum, yum."

You can change the word at the end of the sentence from "Yum, yum, yum" to other phrases, such as "Chew, chew, chew," "Good, good baby" or "Oh, boy!"

This is a fun game that develops fine motor skills.

The Tearing Game

Purpose: Developing fine motor skills

This is a good game to play in the kitchen, where you can give close supervision. Babies really enjoy tearing things.

Gather together old magazines, tissue paper, wrapping paper and foil. Each provides an interesting tearing experience because the textures and sounds are different.

Show the baby how to tear and drop into a box. Babies do like to put things in their mouths, so keep a close watch.

Wad up a piece of paper into a ball and throw it. Show the baby how and let him/her try it. (If the baby cannot make the ball, make it and give it to him/her to throw.)

Three Little Ducks

Purpose: Fine motor development

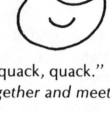

Three little ducks went out to play,
(hold up three fingers)
Under a bridge and far away.
(wiggle finger like swimming)
And the Mommy duck said "Quack, quack, quack."
(form duck bill—hold four fingers together and meet thumb)
Two little ducks came swimming back.
(hold up two fingers and wiggle back).

Two little ducks went out to play,
(hold up two fingers)
Under a bridge and far away.
(wiggle finger like swimming)
And the Daddy duck said "Quack, quack, quack."
(form duck bill—hold four fingers together and meet thumb)
One little duck came swimming back.
(hold up one finger and wiggle back)

One little duck went out to play,
(hold up one finger)
Under a bridge and far away.
(wiggle finger like swimming)
"Where are the baby ducks?" Mommy and Daddy said.
(form duck bill—hold four fingers together and meet thumb)
"We miss them." *(sadly)*
And three little ducks came swimming back.
(three fingers wiggling).

44

Two Little Hot Dogs

Purpose: Having fun, learning about safety

Two little hot dogs frying in a pan,
(lie on the floor on your back)
The grease got hot and one went BAM!
(wiggle around on the floor)

One little hot dog frying in the pan,
(lie on the floor on your back)
One went POP! and one went BAM!
(wiggle around on the floor)

No little hot dogs frying in the pan,
The grease got hot and the pan went BAM!
(wiggle around on the floor)

Each time you say "BAM!" hold baby close and give a big kiss.

Pots and Pans Band

Purpose: Having fun

Get out some pots, pans, plastic bowls, wooden spoons, metal spoons and anything else you can think of to make music.

Sit on the floor with the baby and start banging spoons into pots, pots together, spoons together, etc.

Give a spoon and a pot to the baby and let him/her copy you.

Sing the following (to the tune of "Mary Had a Little Lamb").

Pots and pans are fun to play,
Fun to play, fun to play.
Pots and pans are fun to play.
Let's make music.

Laughing
and
Having Fun
Games

Balance Game

Purpose: To experience movement

Take the baby and put him/her on a bed. While the baby is lying on the bed, gently bounce the mattress.

Now, hold the baby by the arms and jump him/her up and down on the bed.

Lie beside the baby. Gently bounce the mattress and cuddle the baby and talk to him/her.

This game encourages balance stimulation.

One, Two, Three

Purpose: Motor development

Play this game with your baby lying on a pillow on the bed, facing you. Grasp baby's fingers as you hold his/her hands and begin counting.

"Are you ready to stand up? Here we go!"
"One!" *(pronounced "wwwwuuuunnnn")*
"Two!" *(pronounced "ttttooooooooo")*
"Three!" *(pronounced "threeeeeee")*

On the count of three, slowly help the baby to a standing position without letting go of his/her hands.

The baby thinks this is great fun and easily learns to count to three. He/she will also learn to anticipate something great when the count of three is reached.

Follow the Bee

Purpose: Developing visual skills

Sit in a comfortable chair with your baby in your arms. Hold your finger in the air and make a buzzing sound while moving your finger around in the air.

The baby's eyes should follow your "bee." Land the "bee" on the baby with a slight tickle. Repeat this over and over.

Next, take the baby's finger and hold it in the air. Move it around as you did your finger and land it on your cheek.

Babies enjoy this very much.

The Spider Game

Purpose: Fine motor development

This game is not only fun but will begin to develop your baby's fine motor skills.

You and baby lie on the floor on your tummies, facing each other.

Make your fingers crawl like a spider. Make them disappear. Wiggle them. Play the game with the baby's fingers.

Say the following poem and do the actions.

See the little spider,
Crawling right by you.
Here it comes!
There it goes!
Good-bye, spider.
Coming by again,
On your hand,
On your nose.
Good-bye, spider.

Where Are Baby's Hands?

Purpose: Cognitive and motor skills

Play a hand-clapping game with your baby. Sit on the floor with the baby facing you. Put a blanket over your lap. Say the following poem to your baby as you clap the baby's hands.

Clap your hands, one-two-three.
Play a clapping game with me.
Now your hands have gone away.
Find your hands so we can play.

On the words "Now your hands have gone away," put the baby's hands under the blanket. On the words "Find your hands so we can play," bring out the baby's hands from under the blanket.

It's fun to wait to say the last line—it makes it more of a surprise.

Open, Shut Them

Purpose: Developing fine motor skills

Open, shut them;
Open, shut them.
Let your hands go "clap."
Open, shut them;
Open, shut them.
Put them in your lap.

Creep them, creep them;
Creep them, creep them;
Right up to your chin.
Open up
Your little mouth,
But do not let them in.

There are many versions of this popular finger play. It's very nice just to do it as a poem. I particularly like this version for very young children for two reasons: it is short and it has a surprise ending.

Say the poem and do the actions as the baby watches.

When you creep to your chin, it's easiest to creep starting at your waist. Slow down the pace on the words "Open up your little mouth." Wait a second as if you are going to put your fingers in your mouth, then say very quickly, "But do not let them in" as you put your hands behind your back.

The baby will soon try to imitate your actions.

Be prepared for lots of laughter.

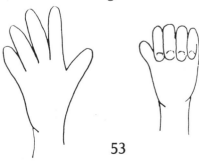

Huff and Puff

Purpose: Language development

String a piece of twine between the backs of two chairs. Fold a large piece of tissue paper in half and hang it over the twine to form the "wall." Cut the tissue paper into lengthwise strips so that the wolf can blow its way into the house.

Now, tell the story of "The Three Little Pigs." When you get to "And he huffed and he puffed," encourage your child to act out the words.

To Market, To Market

Purpose: Bonding and having fun

Sit with the baby on your knees facing you. Hold the baby by the waist until he/she is old enough to hold onto your hands like reins.

To market, to market, to buy a fat pig,
(bounce your knees up and down like a horse)
Home again, home again, jiggity jig.

To market, to market, to buy a fat hog,
(bounce your knees up and down like a horse)
Home again, home again, jiggity jog.

To market, to market, to buy a new gown,
(bounce your knees up and down like a horse)
Home again, home again,
Whoops! The horse fell down.
(straighten your legs and let the child slip down your legs).

Looking Through the Window

Purpose: Having fun

Take a cardboard box (a shoebox works well) and cut two holes in one side. On the opposite side, cut out a window.

Show the child how to look through the holes. While the child is looking through the holes, you can look through the window. What fun to see a familiar face!

Put your finger through the window and wiggle it as the child looks at it. The child will soon learn to look through one side and put things in the window with his/her other hand.

This is a wonderful game that babies really enjoy.

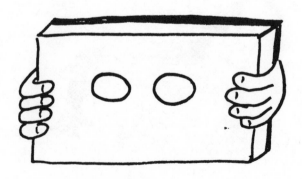

Peek-a-Boo

Purpose: Bonding and having fun

Play "Peek-a-Boo" with your baby. There are many ways to play the game.

Cover your eyes with your hands.

Place the baby's hands over his/her eyes.

Use a blanket between you and the baby. Peek out at the side, at the top and at the bottom of the blanket.

Use a large toy or doll to peek around.

Use a washcloth or a towel.

Put the baby on the bed. Use a lightweight blanket over his/her body and lift it up and down as you peek under it. It will also create a pleasant breeze on the baby's body.

Pat-a-Cake

Purpose: Fine motor development

This is a favorite poem that your baby will never tire of.

Pat-a-cake, pat-a-cake,
(clap hands together)
Baker's man.
Bake me a cake as fast as you can.
Roll it and pat it
And mark it with a "B,"
(trace the letter on your hand)
And put it in the oven
(pretend to close the oven door)
For baby and me.
(point to the baby, then yourself)

First say the poem and do the actions. Next, say the poem and move the baby's hands for the actions. Soon the baby will imitate you and be able to do the actions alone.

Instead of saying the letter "B," you can say the baby's name.

Choo-Choo

Purpose: Balance and having fun

Get a large beach towel and put it on the floor. Sit the baby on the towel and very slowly pull the baby across the floor on the towel.

Pretend with the baby that he/she is riding in something. If it's a car, make a car sound. If it's an airplane, make an airplane sound. If it's a train, make a "choo-choo" sound.

Even though babies do not understand the mode of transportation, they enjoy making the sounds.

Blowing Bubbles

Purpose: Enjoyment

An inexpensive jar of bubbles will provide hours of giggles and fun for you and your toddler.

Blow bubbles outside on a calm day and a windy day.

Form bubbles by moving the round bubble wand through the air (instead of blowing through it).

See how many bubbles you can catch on your blowing wand.

How many bubbles can you see in the bubbles?

Blow bubbles in front of a fan.

Catch some bubbles—try to catch all of them before they reach the ground. Stomp on them! Where do bubbles go when they pop?

Teach your toddler to blow bubbles—this helps language development.

Enjoy watching your cat or dog play with bubbles.

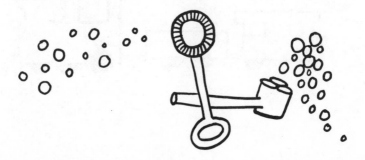

Where's the Music?

Purpose: Developing listening skills

Take a musical toy that the baby is familiar with and wind it up. Hide it somewhere in the room while it's playing.

Get on the floor with the baby and say, "Where's the music?" Start crawling with the baby to see if the baby can find the music.

This game is so much fun for babies, they will want to play it again and again.

61

Can You Catch Me?

Purpose: Having fun

Crawl on the floor with your baby. Say, "Can you catch me?" Crawl ahead of the baby with excitement so that he/she comes after you. Be sure and let the baby catch you.

Now, switch roles and say, "I'm going to get you!" Let the baby crawl ahead.

This is great fun for babies and they will play the game over and over.

When you "get" the baby, give him/her a big hug.

The Exercise Game

Purpose: Developing gross motor skills

Hold the baby's hands as you face each other. Sing the following song (to the tune of "Farmer in the Dell").

*Jumping up and down,
We're jumping up and down.
Getting lots of exercise,
We're jumping up and down.*

Start changing the words with the first line of the verse (always keeping line three the same).

*Bend and touch our toes,
We bend and touch our toes.
Getting lots of exercise,
We bend and touch our toes.*

Some other ideas are: stretching way up high, running in our place, twisting side to side.

One Little Elephant

Purpose: Having fun

Enjoy this silly poem with your baby.

One little elephant went out to play
(walk around bent over with arm in front of face for elephant's trunk)
Out on a spider web one day.
(pretend to walk carefully on a spider web).
He had such enormous fun
That he called for another elephant to come.
(motion for "another elephant"—the baby)
Too many elephants. . . . CRASH!!
(fall down with baby)

This next variation teaches colors.

One little elephant went out to play
Out on the busy street one day.
He had such enormous fun
That he called for a yellow car to come.
Too many cars. . . . CRASH!!

Use toy cars and change the colors of the cars. You can also say "He had such enormous fun that he called for a yellow car to come, he called for a red car to come, he called for a blue car to come," and get all the cars together before you say "Too many cars. . . . CRASH!!"

Abracadabra

Purpose: Visual discrimination

On large pieces of paper, trace around objects familiar to your child. Some examples are blocks, silverware, favorite toys and cookie cutters. Put the objects that you have traced around into a box.

Say the following poem with your child.

*Abracadabra, one, two, three;
Look in the box, what do I see?*

The child then picks an object and tries to match it to the outline that you have drawn.

The poem makes this game very special. Closing your eyes when you say the poem makes it even more fun.

Little Fish

Purpose: Bonding and fun

Say the following poem.

Little fish, little fish
(Put palms together to form fish)
Goes out to play.
(Move hands back and forth as though swimming)
Wiggles his fins and swims away.

He swims and swims in the water bright,
Opens his mouth
(Open hands [mouth])
And takes a bite.

Mmm, mmm, tastes good!!
(Rub your tummy)

Looking for a Rainbow

Purpose: Sensory development

There are many things to do with a garden hose. Spray the water in a high arc and let the children run under it.

★ Shoot the water in a stream a few inches off the ground so they can jump over it.

★ Raise the stream and have them crawl under it.

★ Wiggle the water back and forth like a snake.

★ Let the children water the flowers and grass. Make a mud or sand puddle.

★ Hang the hose over a tree limb or swing set and let the water run in a steady stream.

★ Look for a rainbow when you spray the water overhead.

Join in the fun—let your child spray you, too!

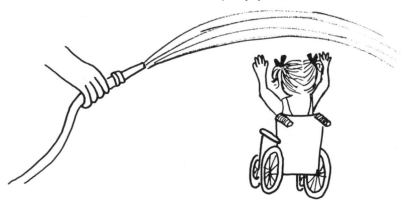

The Sand Game

Purpose: Encouraging imagination

A sandbox or sand table is a wonderful toy to have for young children. Many skills can be developed while playing in the sand. Here are some activities that you can do.

Fill and empty cups and containers.

Make roads and drive "cars" over them.

Bury your bare feet in the sand.

Bury toys and find them.

Bath
and
Dressing
Games

Baby's Bath

Purpose: Bonding

For a relaxing change of pace, take a warm bath with your baby. Hold your baby as you rock back and forth.

Sing to the baby as you rock. Make up words ("We are taking a bath together," "I love my little baby, baby, baby," etc.) and melodies. The song is not important, the bonding is.

Washing Baby

Purpose: Identifying body parts

Use bathtime to further develop your baby's self-concept. Sing songs about the different body parts as you wash them.

Sing the following song (to the tune of "London Bridge Is Falling Down").

*Head and shoulders, knees and toes,
Knees and toes, knees and toes.
Head and shoulders, knees and toes,
Eyes and ears and mouth and nose.*

Sing the song as you wash each part of the body and identify it in the song at the same time.

71

Sweet Baby Mine

Purpose: *Tactile enjoyment and bonding*

Play this game any time you dress your baby. It's especially nice after a bath.

Massage and stroke the baby; kiss, cuddle and blow air on the baby's body. Tell the baby that you love him/her. Talk about the parts of the body you are massaging.

Say the following poem as you are dressing the baby.

"(Mama or Daddy) loves you so, sweet baby mine.
You are so soft and nice to cuddle.
I'll wiggle your nose and ten of your toes,
Then go round and round on your nice soft tummy.
Now for a kiss, sweet baby mine.
You are so soft and nice to cuddle."

Baby's Fingers

Purpose: Learning body parts

When you are dressing a baby you have the perfect opportunity to talk about the different parts of the body.

Take the baby's fingers and gently touch each one. As you do this, say in a sing-song voice, "This is (child's name) finger." Then take the baby's hand and put it on your finger. In the same sing-song voice, say "This is (Mommy's or Daddy's) finger."

This game not only develops body-part awareness and vocabulary, but it gives adult and child an opportunity to bond.

Hello, Hands

Purpose: Visual stimulation

Take a pair of the baby's socks and cut holes in them for fingers to stick out. Decorate with bright colors, interesting shapes or faces. Put the sock on the baby's hands for him/her to look at, talk to, enjoy.

Remember: babies put their hands in their mouths, so be sure that any decoration is safe.

Follow the Toy

Purpose: *Developing controlled eye movement*

Attract the baby's attention by shaking a rattle about a foot from baby's face. When the baby fixes his/her eyes on the rattle, slowly move it in a half circle.

Next, do the same thing with a speaking toy. By changing the object you will hold the infant's attention for a longer period of time.

This game develops eye coordination.

Shoe Game

Purpose: Having fun and experimenting with language

This is a poem to say when you are putting on the baby's shoes.

Shoe the old horse,
Shoe the old mare,
But let the little colt
Go bare, bare, bare.

When you say the last line, the shoe should be tied. Then tap the sole of the foot each time you say the words "bare, bare, bare." The baby will begin to look forward to the tapping part.

Wash Those Toes

Purpose: Learning body parts

Sing this song (to the tune of "Here We Go 'Round the Mulberry Bush") to your baby as you give him/her a bath.

*This is the way we wash our toes,
Wash our toes, wash our toes.
This is the way we wash our toes.
I love you.*

Repeat with other body parts: "This is the way we wash our feet," "This is the way we wash our hands," etc.

Zip, Zip, Zip

Purpose: Having fun while changing a diaper

Diapering a baby gets harder as the baby gets older.
Having a special poem to say will keep the baby's
attention.

Zip, zip, zip, off it goes!
I see baby without clothes.
Zip, zip, what do I see?
Diaper on, one-two-three!

Trying to say the word "zip" is great fun for the baby.

Balloon Game

Purpose: Making discoveries; language and motor skills

Fill up a small balloon with ¼ cup of water. Tie a knot in the balloon. Show your baby how it changes shape as you squeeze and wiggle it.

Now for the fun: let the baby experiment. The baby will soon discover that it will bounce when you drop it and wiggle when you roll it.

Do the same thing with two balloons of different colors. Each time you drop the balloon or squeeze it, identify the color by name. Each time you give the baby a balloon, say the color as you give it to the baby.

So-o-o Big!

Purpose: Self-awareness

This is best played on a flat surface while the baby is lying on his/her back.

Reach out for your baby to grasp your fingers. Gently raise the baby to a sitting position and say, "Baby (child's name) is SO-O-O big!" If the baby cannot hold onto your hand, place your hands over his/her fingers.

As the baby grows older, say "Up SO-O-O high and down we go!" Bring the baby up and then back down.

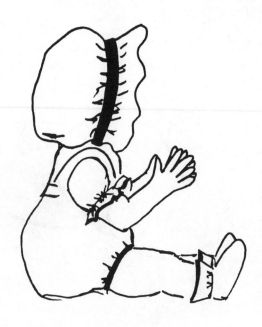

Ten Little Toesies

Purpose: Bonding and counting

Sing this to the tune of "Ten Little Indians."

*One little, two little, three little toesies,
Four little, five little, six little toesies,
Seven little, eight little, nine little toesies,
Ten little tickle toes.*

*Ten little, nine little, eight little toesies,
Seven little, six little, five little toesies,
Four little, three little, two little toesies,
One little tickle toe.*

In the bath or out of the bath, your baby will enjoy this song. As you sing, gently touch each toe or finger. When you come to the last line, you can splash the water, turn your baby around in the water or make up your own idea.

When you are drying the baby, pat each toe or finger as you dry them and at the end, again, do something different. A nice big hug is a fun thing to do!

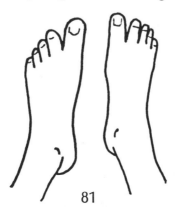

81

Chin Chopper

Purpose: Language development

Hold your baby and talk softly to him/her. Give the
baby an opportunity to talk back to you.

Then, play a face-tapping game. Gently tap each part of
the face and say the following words.

*This is baby's chin chopper,
Chin chopper, chin chopper.
This is baby's chin chopper.
How are you today?*

Follow the same pattern with eye peeper, nose
dropper, mouth eater, brow bender.

You can make up words for other parts of the body.
For example, finger toucher, toe wiggler, etc.

What Are You Wearing?

Purpose: Vocabulary building

When you are dressing your child, talk about the color of the clothes. Sing a little song about the clothes.

(Child's name) has a sweater,
And it is blue.
(Child's name) has a sweater,
And it is (let the child answer "Blue").

(Child's name) has a shirt,
And it is white.
(Child's name) has a shirt,
And it is (let the child answer "White").

This is also a good opportunity to recite the nursery rhyme "Diddle, Diddle, Dumpling."

*Diddle, diddle, dumpling,
my son John
Went to bed with his
stockings on.
One shoe off and one shoe
on,
Diddle, diddle, dumpling,
my son John.*

Dressing time is a wonderful bonding time.

Water Fun

Purpose: Sensory, cognitive and motor development

There are many things to do with your baby when you fill a bathtub with water:

★ Practice pouring

★ Discover what sinks or floats

★ Use an eggbeater in the water

★ Squeeze a sponge in the water

★ Pretend to wash dishes

Art
and
Singing
Games

This Little Piggy

Purpose: Bonding

*This little piggy went to market
And this little piggy stayed home.
And this little piggy had roast beef
And this little piggy had none.
And this little piggy went
"Wee wee wee wee wee wee wee wee"
All the way home.*

Babies love to explore their fingers and toes. Touch each finger or toe as you say the poem. Before you sing the "Wee wee wee" part, slow down and build suspense. Then say the last line faster than the rest.

On the "Wee wee wee" part you can do many things: tickle the baby, dance around holding the baby, or gently shake the baby's hand or foot.

Another variation is to say the "Wee wee wee" part in different kinds of voices—high, low, happy, sad, etc.

Substitute the baby's name for the word "piggy."

Sing Sing Sing

Purpose: Language and listening skills

Sing to your baby about anything—describe your surroundings, describe car trips, cleaning the house—wherever you are and whatever you are doing.

Here are some sample ideas to sing to the tune of "Row, Row, Row Your Boat."

*Let's go to the store
On this rainy day.
We will buy some food to eat,
Then go home again.*

*Let's clean up the room;
Lots of things to do.
Make it look so clean and bright,
Now it looks just right.*

*Let's go to the kitchen.
Are you hungry now?
Apples, peas, bread and jelly,
And some milk to drink.*

Are You Sleeping?

Purpose: Bonding

Are you sleeping, are you sleeping,
Little (child's name), little (child's name)?
Now it's time to wake up,
Now it's time to wake up,
Ding, ding, dong. Ding, ding, dong.

This is a good peek-a-boo song. Cover your eyes as you say "Are you sleeping, are you sleeping?" Fill in the child's name on the second line and take your hands away from your eyes. When you say the words "Now it's time to wake up," take the baby's hands and pull him/her upward. Move the baby's hands up and down (as though ringing a bell) on "Ding, ding, dong."

You can sing the song another way: put the baby's hands over his/her eyes and instead of "Are you sleeping?" say "Are you hiding?" Instead of "Little (child's name)," say "Yes, I am." The rest of the song stays the same.

Where Is Thumbkin?

Purpose: Fine motor development

Where is Thumbkin? *Where is Ringman?*
Where is Thumbkin? *Where is Ringman?*
Here I am, here I am. *Here I am, here I am.*
How are you today, sir? *How are you today, sir?*
Very well, I thank you. *Very well, I thank you.*
Run away, run away. *Run away, run away.*

Where is Pointer? *Where is Pinky?*

Where is Middleman? *Where's the whole family?*

Babies adore this popular singing game. Start with your hands behind your back. Bring out the thumb on one hand on the first "Where is Thumbkin?" and then the thumb on the other hand on the second "Where is Thumbkin?"

Wiggle one thumb on "How are you today, sir?" and the other on "Very well, I thank you," then put them behind your back one at a time on the words "Run away."

89

Lazy Mary

Purpose: Waking-up song

Lazy Mary, will you get up,
Will you get up, will you get up?
Lazy Mary, will you get up
This cold and frosty morning?

Singing this popular children's song is a lovely way to
wake your baby. Substitute the name of your baby for
"Mary" and substitute the word "lazy" with words like
"pretty," "silly," "funny" and "happy."

If the baby is lying down when you sing the song, hold
the baby's hands as you slowly raise him/her up. If you
are holding the baby as you sing the song, rock back
and forth slowly as you sing.

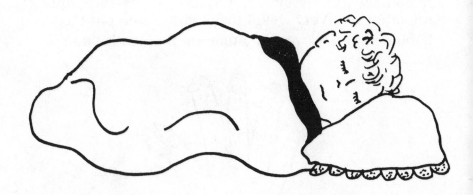

One, Two, One, Two

Purpose: Enjoying music

Play some instrumental music. Hold your baby and sway back and forth or dance around the floor. Show the baby different kinds of things to do with the music—clapping hands, stomping feet, swinging arms and marching.

Play some music with vocals. Sing "La, la, la" and let the baby imitate you. Pick out a particular word in the song and sing it to the baby each time you hear that word. You will be amazed at how quickly the baby will anticipate the word. (This is also a wonderful game for listening skills.)

Play loud music and soft music, fast music and slow music, high sounds and low sounds.

I See Something

Purpose: Identifying objects

Collect a baby bottle, a ball and a toy of one color (for example, a toy car). Sing the following to the tune of "Frere Jacques."

I see something, I see something
Used to drink, used to drink.
It is tall and round,
It is just for baby.
What is it? What is it?
(Bottle)

I see something, I see something
Used to play, used to play.
It is very round,
It will roll all over.
What is it? What is it?
(Ball)

I see something, I see something.
It can go, it can go.
It is green and shiny,
And the horn goes "beep-beep."
What is it? What is it?
(Toy car)

This is a wonderful game for nonverbal children because all they have to do is to point to or pick up the particular object.

You can take this song and make up words to fit anything in the baby's environment.

92

The Shape Game

Purpose: Creativity and fine motor skills

You will need a large piece of paper for drawing and a blue crayon.

Sit with your child at a table or on the floor. Take the crayon and draw a circle on the paper, then put the crayon in the child's hand and guide his/her hand in making a circle. Say to the child, "What a pretty picture."

Next, take the crayon in the child's hand and draw a different shape. When you are through, say "What a pretty picture." Experiment with different shapes—zig-zag lines, free movement lines, etc.

Babies love this game and, interestingly enough, will want to take turns. The baby will probably give the crayon to you and say, "You do it."

Each time you play this game, it's a good idea to use a different color of crayon so the child can begin to learn to identify colors. (It's also a good idea to use "fat" crayons—they are easier for little hands to hold.)

This Old Man

Purpose: Counting

This old man, he played one,
He played nick-nack on my thumb.
With a nick-nack, paddy-whack,
Give a dog a bone,
This old man came rolling home.

Two—on my shoe
Three—on my knee
Four—on my door
Five—on a hive
Six—on some sticks
Seven—all the way to Heaven
Eight—on my gate
Nine—on my spine
Ten—once again

This is a wonderful spoon-banging song. On the part that says "This old man came rolling home," take the baby's fists and roll them over each other.

It is also fun to do actions to the rhyming word—touch shoe, touch knee, knock on door, etc.

Paint the World

Purpose: Language and fun

Give your child a paintbrush and a pail of water, then go outside and let your child have fun.

Sing this song to the tune of "Mulberry Bush."

This is the way we paint the house,
Paint the house, paint the house.
This is the way we paint the house
Every single day.

Let your child paint the house with water.

Sing the same song about the sidewalk, the porch, the mailbox, the car, whatever won't be hurt by being "painted" with water.

95

Working with Clay

Purpose: Fine motor skills and creativity

Here are some activities for you and your baby to do with modeling clay.

★ Help your child make balls and snakes.

★ Talk about colors of clay. Mix colors together.

★ Form shapes with clay—circles, triangles, squares.

★ Make letters.

★ Press or roll with rolling pin to make a flat surface. Make patterns with objects (blocks, toys, comb, rocks). Cut with cookie cutters.

★ Make two objects and compare as large and small.

★ Feel the temperature of the clay before it is worked (cool), then work with it and feel its temperature (warm). Talk about why it feels different (feel temperature of hands against cheeks).

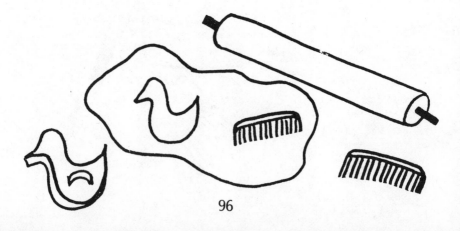

Ring Around the Rosy

Purpose: Bonding

Ring around the rosy,
A pocket full of posy.
Ashes, ashes, we all fall down.

I have found this game to be a great favorite with my baby. If your baby can walk, hold his/her hands and walk in a circle, falling down at the appropriate time.

If your baby cannot walk, hold him and walk around in a circle, then sit down on a chair with a gentle movement.

It's also fun to play this game holding a stuffed animal, making the animal fall down.

Pumpkin Printing

Purpose: Creating design

This is a good game to begin after Halloween.

Cut shapes from the rind of your pumpkin—a square, triangle, rectangle, circle and irregular shapes.

Dip the shapes into tempera paint and make print designs on large pieces of paper. As you print the design, tell its name.

Give your child a shape. Tell the child the name of the shape and then let him/her make designs all over the paper with the shape. Continue doing this with the nameable shapes. When you get to the irregular shapes, make up names for them.

Many fruits and vegetables make excellent designs, such as carrots, apple slices, potatoes, etc. Sponges are easily cut into shapes for printing.

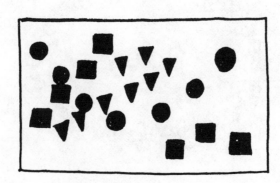

The Shadow Game

Purpose: Science and gross motor development

Go for a walk outside on a sunny day and look for shadows. Look at your own shadow. Move your arms, jump up and down, jump on your baby's shadow and talk about how the shadow got there.

Sing the following song (to the tune of "The Muffin Man") while watching your shadow.

Oh, do you see my shadow go,
My shadow go, my shadow go?
Oh, do you see my shadow go?
It goes along with me.

Oh, do you see my shadow bend,
My shadow bend, my shadow bend?
Oh, do you see my shadow bend?
It bends along with me.

Oh, do you see my shadow jump,

Oh, do you see my shadow run,

99

Find the Other One

Purpose: Visual discrimination

Play a matching game with pairs of things—shoes, mittens, colored napkins, towels, washcloths. Mix up a few pairs and help your child find the pairs that match.

Sing the following song (to the tune of "Frere Jacques"), changing the item and color of description as fits. Start with one pair only, then graduate to more than one.

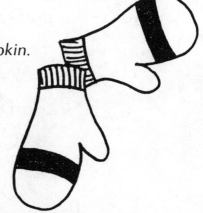

I have a mitten, I have a mitten.
It is red, it is red.
Help me find the other one,
Help me find the other one.
Here it is, here it is.

I have a shoe, I have a shoe.
It is brown, it is brown.
Help me find the other one,
Help me find the other one.
Here it is, here it is.

I have a napkin, I have a napkin.
It is yellow, it is yellow.
Help me find the other one,
Help me find the other one.
Here it is, here it is.

Paint with Your Feet

Purpose: Fun

Spread a large piece of paper outside. Have a large shallow tray with large sponges in the tray. Pour tempera paint on the sponges.

Use your feet as paintbrushes. Hold your child's hand and show him/her how to dip a foot into the paint.

Walk across the paper, holding the child's hand in case it's a little slippery.

Use different colors of paint. Dip the wheels of a washable toy in the paint and see what kind of "footprints" it will leave. Put paint on a ball and roll it across the paper.

You can also make "handprints."

Special Bonding Games

Talking Toys

Purpose: Grasping, visual and tactile practice

Find a quiet time to play this game with your baby.
Place many different stuffed toys and animals around
the crib. Some of the toys should be small enough for
the baby to grasp.

Hold a toy in front of the baby and move it around. As
you move it, make it "talk." The baby will try to grasp
it. When the baby does grasp it, he/she will feel
successful.

Do this with many different sizes, shapes and textures
of toys. Give them different voices so the baby can
hear different sounds.

This is an excellent game for fine motor development
and listening skills.

Kick, Kick, Kick

Purpose: Gross motor development

Babies enjoy kicking and lifting their legs. As you know, they get their toes in their mouths at a very young age.

To help the baby practice kicking, find items to place at the baby's feet such as stuffed animals, your hands, squeaky toys, etc.

Hold up a pillow at the baby's feet and let him/her kick at that.

Fly, Baby, Fly

Purpose: Bonding

Sit on the floor with the baby facing you. Support the baby's body with your hands placed firmly around the baby's chest and under the arms.

"Are you ready to fly in the sky?" you ask. "Here we go—one, two, threeeee!"

On the count of three, begin lifting the baby up as you roll backwards on your back. You are now lying down and holding the baby "high in the sky." Say words like, "Fly, baby, fly!" "Whee!" and whatever else you think of.

This game is also good for the parent—it strengthens back muscles.

Stroke the Baby

Purpose: Increasing body awareness

Find different objects to stroke your baby with—a blanket, silk, a feather or a cotton ball.

Hum softly as you stroke the baby. (Lullabies are nice.)

Now, rub the baby's fingers and toes one at a time as you hum softly. The baby will enjoy this very much.

Next, take the objects that you used and stroke the baby's fingers and toes, one at a time, with each object.

This is a lovely bonding game that encourages interaction with an adult.

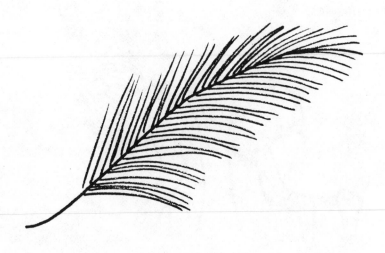

Exploring

Purpose: Exploring

Lie down on the bed and put the baby on your chest.
First, hold the baby firmly and say loving things like "I
love you," "What a sweet boy/girl," etc.

Next, help the baby explore the different parts of your
body. When the baby touches your nose, say the word
"nose." When the baby touches your hair, say "hair."
The idea is to let the baby explore.

Hold the baby up over your head and say loving things
while looking into each other's eyes.

Bumping Noses

Purpose: Having fun

Sit the baby in your lap, facing you. Say "Boo!" three times. As you say the word, move your head toward the baby's head and on the third "Boo!" bump noses with the baby. (If you say the last one a little louder, it makes the game even more fun.)

Keep repeating this over and over. Change the tone of your voice as you repeat—sometimes use a high voice, sometimes a low voice, sometimes a whisper with the last "Boo!" at voice level. (Be careful not to shout— that might scare the baby.)

Coos and Hugs

Purpose: Language development

Infants have a language all their own—cooing. When an infant sees something of interest, they will respond with a coo.

Play a cooing game with your baby. Hold a brightly colored object in front of your baby's eyes. When the baby coos, you respond with a coo and then a hug. You will soon learn what pleases your baby.

When babies learn that their sounds are pleasing to another, they will make more sounds. Chances are they will be early talkers as a result.

Whoops, Johnny

Purpose: Language and fine motor development

Take your baby's hand in yours. Starting with the thumb, touch each finger with your pointer finger and say "Johnny." After saying "Johnny" when you get to the ring finger, slide down that finger and up the little finger, saying "Whoops!" and then "Johnny" when you reach the tip of the little finger.

Reverse the game, starting with the little finger—say "Johnny," then "Whoops!" as you slide down the little finger and up the ring finger, saying "Johnny" again as you reach the tip. Then finish the fingers.

The game will sound like this: "Johnny, Johnny, Johnny, Johnny, Whoops! Johnny; Whoops, Johnny! Johnny, Johnny, Johnny,."

Substitute your child's name for "Johnny."

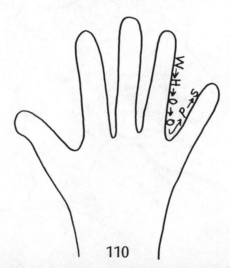

110

Feels Good

Purpose: Developing tactile discrimination

Hold your baby in your arms and go on a texture walk around the house. Help your baby feel the objects as you describe them.

Find and describe things that are rough, sticky, smooth, soft, hard, prickly, silky, tickly, bumpy, cold (inside the refrigerator).

Play the same game outside, in the car, at a store, etc.

This is a wonderful vocabulary builder.

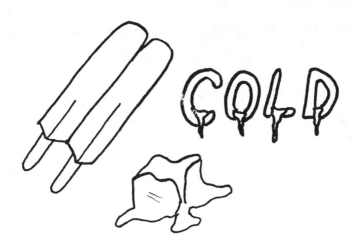

M-m-m Nice

Purpose: A tactile experience

Put the baby in a sitting position for this activity. Put the tactile materials in a "feely box" and set it aside.

Use a fur piece to show the baby a stroking motion. Pat the infant's cheek with the fur and rub it along the baby's arm or leg. Murmur softly as you do this—"M-m-m nice," "So-so soft" or similar words.

Give the baby the fur piece and see what he/she does with it. Encourage the baby to feel it by petting, stroking or rubbing it against parts of the body. Use tissue paper to demonstrate crushing and foam rubber for squeezing.

Making sounds also encourages language development.

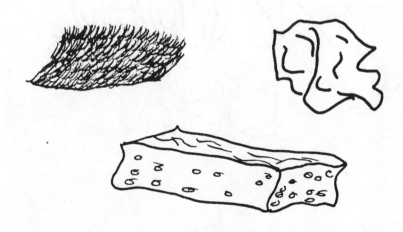

Color Walk

Purpose: Recognizing colors

Go on a color walk with your baby. Select a certain color toy and take it with you.

Find one or two objects in each room that are the same color. As the child gets older, you can find more objects.

Talk about what you've found—for example, "Daddy's yellow tie is the same color as your yellow ball" or "Mommy's blue blouse is the same color as your blue block."

Another variation of this game is to carry a laundry basket around, collecting toys and other objects of the same color.

Sharing Game

Purpose: Sharing

Sit on the floor opposite your baby. Hand the baby an object, saying, "This is for the baby." After the baby has had a chance to touch it, look at it and explore it, say "Will you give it to me, please?" The baby will then give the object back to you. Now, repeat the game.

If the baby does not want to return the object, it's okay to gently remove it. Once the baby understands that it is a game, he/she will become more trusting.

Baby Bunny

Purpose: Enjoyment

Say the poem and do the actions with your hands and fingers.

Here are the baby bunny ears,
(hold up bunny)
And here is his little pink nose.
(touch bunny's nose)
This is the way he hippity hops
(hop the bunny)
Everywhere he goes.

This is the way the baby bunny crawls,
(bunny crawls up to your chin and cuddles under your chin; you turn your head to the side as if to hug the bunny)
Shuts his eyes and goes to sleep,
(close your eyes)
With his little feet tucked in.
(pet the bunny)

Bunny nose

Two Little Dickey Birds

Purpose: Fine motor development

Say the following poem and do the actions.

Two little dickey birds, sitting on a hill, *(close hands
and stick up thumbs)*
One named Jack *(bring right thumb forward)*
And one named Jill. *(bring left thumb forward)*
Fly away, Jack. *(fly right thumb to back)*
Fly away, Jill. *(fly left thumb to back)*
Come back, Jack. *(bring right thumb back)*
Come back, Jill. *(bring right thumb back)*

Another idea is to wet your thumb and stick a small
piece of tissue on for birds.

Finger puppets are also nice to use with this finger
play.

Flashlight Fun

Purpose: Developing fine motor skills

Take a flashlight and shine it on different places in the room—on the wall, on the door, on the floor, under the covers, etc. Each time you shine the light on an object, say its name: "This is the wall." "This is the doorknob."

Show your child how to turn the flashlight on and off. Let the child shine it on an object and you tell the name of the object.

Give the child directions: "Shine the light on the ceiling." "Shine the light on the window." The child will understand, even though he/she might not have the language capability of saying the words.

Make a bird shadow: crossing your wrists with palms facing you, extend your fingers (the wings) and touch the fleshy part of the thumbs (to form the bird's head). Move your hands to make the bird "fly."

Look at pictures in a book or magazine using the flashlight.

Eensy-Weensy Spider

Purpose: *Language development*

Say the poem "Eensy-Weensy Spider" with your child and teach your child the following actions.

Eensy-weensy spider went up the water spout. *(make fingers crawl into the air)*
Down came the rain and washed the spider out. *(make fingers go downward like falling rain)*
Out came the sun and dried up all the rain *(make a great big circle with arms to indicate the sun)*
And the eensy-weensy spider went up the spout again. *(crawl fingers upward as in the first line)*

Do the actions for the baby and soon the baby will be imitating you.

Now, say the poem in different ways, always keeping the actions the same. Try these ways: say "La, la, la" or "Ooh, ooh, ooh," hum, whistle, use first-letter sounds, do the actions without sound.

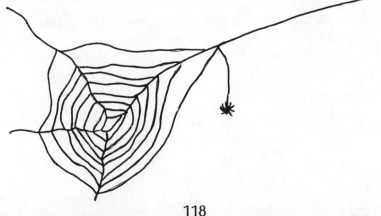

Guidelines for Growth

Motor, Auditory and Visual Skills

Baby holds up head

Grasps a rattle or toy

Rolls from back to side

Sits with hand support

Pulls to sitting position, holding adult fingers

Follows moving objects with eyes

Focuses eyes on small object

Begins to reach for objects

Picks up block

Transfers object from hand to hand

Reacts with startle to sharp noise

Turns head in direction of bell

Turns head toward voice sound

Responds to voice with activity

Language and Cognitive Skills

Babbles and coos

Gurgles on seeing others

Makes simple sounds— "Ah," "Ooh"

Says one sound repeatedly

Smiles, chuckles, laughs

Attempts a variety of sounds

Makes sounds when attended

Smiles in response to attention

Shows eagerness by making sounds

Fusses when a favored toy is removed

Responds differently to handling

Reacts to sight of toy

Shows awareness of change in routine

Attempts to repeat doing things enjoyed before

Reacts to strangers

Self-Concept Skills

Inspects own hands

Brings things to own mouth

Focuses eyes on own moving hands

Smiles at mirror images

Vocalizes at mirror image

Anticipates feeding

Plays unattended for 10 minutes

Picks up spoon

Feeds self cracker

Holds bottle part of the time

Lifts cup with handle

Looks directly at person's face

Recognizes parent

Reaches for familiar persons

Responds to "Peek-a-boo"

Smiles in response to facial expressions

SIX TO TWELVE MONTHS
Motor, Auditory and Visual Skills

Baby bounces when held in a standing position

Sits unsupported

Pulls pegs from pegboard

Rolls ball while sitting

Crawls rapidly, climbs on stairs

Stands unaided

Moves hand to follow eye focus

Picks up small objects with thumb and finger

Puts a few blocks in a cup

Bangs two blocks together

Looks at pictures in books

Drops small objects into containers

Responds to voice tones and inflections in others

Recognizes familiar words and responds accordingly

Shakes bell in imitation of adult

Stops activity after hearing "No-no"

Shows interest in certain words and gestures

Language and Cognitive Skills

Imitates speech sounds

Babbles rhythmically

Combines two syllables—"Da-da," "Ma-ma"

Imitates sounds of dog, clock, cow, etc.

Expresses first real words other than "Mama" and "Dada"

Attracts attention by making noises

Imitates clapping hands

Waves "Bye-bye"

Follows simple directions

Understands "No"

Shakes head to indicate "No"

Pulls string to obtain a toy

Finds block hidden under cup

Knows meaning of "Dada," "Mama"

Removes block from cup when shown

Squeezes toy to make it squeak

Looks to find toys which have gone out of sight

Seeks or demands attention

Pushes away another's hands to keep a toy

Holds arms in front of face to avoid being washed

Holds arms out to be picked up

Sucks soft foods from spoon

Holds, bites, chews cracker or biscuit

Finger feeds self in part

Drinks from cup with help

Controls drooling

Responds to others' gestures

Plays and enjoys "Patty Cake"

Repeats performance when laughed at

Encourages an audience

Cooperates in dressing by holding arms out

TWELVE TO TWENTY-FOUR MONTHS
Motor, Auditory and Visual Skills

Baby walks independently

Holds two small objects in one hand

Walks up and down stairs with help, hand held

Jumps in place

Kicks large ball

Throws small ball overhand

Recognizes familiar person

Scribbles on paper

Stacks three to six blocks

Turns knobs

Can find objects of the same color, shape or size

Points to distant interesting object outdoors

Turns toward family member whose name is spoken

Understands and follows a simple command

Notices sounds—clock, bell, whistle

Responds rhythmically to music with whole-body activity

Carries out two-step direction

Language and Cognitive Skills

Jabbers with expression

Identifies with pictures in book

Uses single words meaningfully

Names objects when asked, "What's this?"

Uses twenty or more words

Names twenty-five familiar objects

Gestures to make wants known

Names toys

Uses words to make wants known

Combines two different words

Tries to sing

Speaks in simple sentences

Finds familiar objects

Imitates fitting objects into containers

Turns two to three pages of a book at a time

Points to named pictures in a book

Remembers where objects belong

Obtains toy using stick or string

Self-Concept Skills

Demands personal attention

Points to three named body parts

Insists on helping feed self

Names body parts on doll

Claims objects as his own

Refers to self by name

Pulls off socks, mittens

Eats with spoon

Drinks from cup

Attempts washing self

Offers toy but does not release it

Plays independently around another child

Helps parents with simple tasks

Plays contentedly alone if near adults

Enjoys short walks

Asks for food and water when needed

An Invitation

Do you have a special game that you play with your baby?

We will be publishing a second book of games and if you would like to contribute please do the following.

Send a typewritten, double spaced description of your game, the age of your baby, your name, address, city, state, zip code and phone number.

If your game appears in the book, we will print your name and give you a FREE BOOK!!

Send the information to: **Miss Jackie Music Company**
Baby Games
10001 El Monte
Overland Park, Kansas 66207

Game Index by Ages

Twelve to Eighteen Months

Eighteen to Twenty-Four Months

Miss Jackie Music Co.

BOOKS

Great Big Book of Rhythm   **$12.95**
144 pages of ideas using rhythm to teach listening, language, motor and cognitive skills and to strengthen self-concept.

Sniggles, Squirrels and Chicken Pox   **$8.95**
40 delightful songs, words, music and chords plus activities. Originally in *The Instructor* magazine.

Songs to Sing with Babies   **$8.95**
Songs, games and activities to do with babies. Songs for rocking and nursing, cuddling, waking up and getting dressed.

Peanut Butter Activity Book   **$8.95**
Language and movement activities, flannelboard patterns, bulletin board ideas and art activities to go with the record of the same name.

Lollipops and Spaghetti Activity Book   **$8.95**
Dozens of teacher-tested ideas to develop skills. Companion to best-selling record of the same name.

Hello, Rhythm   **$6.95**
47 easy and fun-to-play rhythm games plus nine songs will expand your child's natural sense of rhythm.

Hello, Sound   **$6.95**
Dozens of ideas plus songs to develop reading readiness, listening skills and auditory discrimination.

All About Me/Let's Be Friends   **Set: $10.00**
These two books and 45-rpm record set include sensitive photographs to illustrate the words of these picture song books that celebrate the joys of friendship, sharing and playing together.

RECORDS OR TAPES

Lollipops and Spaghetti $9.95
Mixes valuable learning with songs that are fun to sing
and hear, including "Lollipop Tree" and "On Top of
Spaghetti." (Recorded live.)

Peanut Butter, Tarzan and Roosters $9.95
Songs like "I'm So Mad I Could Scream" teach
important fundamentals (like feelings) and fun.
(Recorded live.)

Sniggles, Squirrels and Chicken Pox, Vol. I $9.95
Recorded in a studio on 24 tracks, this album includes
"Baby Bear's Chicken Pox" and many seasonal songs to
a variety of moods and tempos.

Sniggles, Squirrels and Chicken Pox, Vol. 2 $9.95
Charming songs in many styles of music include
wonderful sound effects along with a variety of
instruments and voices.

Sing Around the World $9.95
Children learn songs from several countries and
participate vigorously. (Recorded live.)

Hello, Rhythm $9.95
Self-directed rhythm songs for a child to listen to and
do with Miss Jackie.

Songs to Sing with Babies $8.95
Songs are sung in the order they appear in the book of
the same name so adult can learn them or baby can
listen. (Cassette only.)

Sing a Jewish Song   Set: $9.95
Recorded live in St. Louis for the Jewish Preschool
Association, this is a participatory, fun recording.

10 Reasons to Subscribe to
Early Childhood Music Newsletter
Every 12-page issue contains:

★ Original music with activities for the classroom

★ Special parents' programs

★ Musical games and exercises

★ Feature articles of interest to early childhood professionals

★ Learning center activities

★ How to play the autoharp

★ Movement activities

★ Book, tape and record reviews

★ Discounts on materials

★ Circle time activities

We all know that using music with children can be a wonderful aid in teaching skills—listening, language, cognitive and motor. In addition, music activities promote self-concept and self-esteem in young children. Shouldn't music be a more prominent part of your curriculum?

YOU DO NOT HAVE TO BE A MUSICIAN TO USE THE IDEAS IN *EARLY CHILDHOOD MUSIC*

This wonderful bimonthly treasure is written with the early childhood professional in mind—not necessarily the teacher who plays a musical instrument. All the ideas can be used by the non-musician or the amateur musician as well as by the trained musician. And what an addition to your classroom effectiveness this newsletter can be!

Yes! I want to subscribe! Enclosed is my check. Put me on your mailing list for *Early Childhood Music* **today!**

	USA	Foreign	Canada
One year (6 issues)	$19.50	$29.50	$22.50
Two year (12 issues)	39.00	59.00	45.00

Name _____

Address _____

City _____ State _____ ZIP _____

Phone _____ Date _____

Mail form and payment to: Amount
Early Childhood Music   Enclosed $_____
Department BG
10001 El Monte, Overland Park, KS 66207

127

About the Author

Better known as "Miss Jackie" to thousands of teachers, parents and children throughout the United States and Canada, Jackie Weissman is a children's concert artist, composer, educator, consultant, national columnist, recording artist and television personality.

She is an adjunct instructor in Early Childhood Education at Emporia (KS) State University and a monthly contributor to the prestigious magazine for teachers, *The Instructor*. She is also on the advisory board of *ECE Teacher* and contributes quarterly.

Jackie Weissman is the author of many books dealing with music, games and young children. She has also produced many recordings (mostly of her own songs) and workshop audio and video tapes that are widely used for teacher training.

"Miss Jackie's" music appears in college texts, elementary music books and learning kits for language, math and social studies. She recently wrote a song for the Campbell Soup Company that is being used nationwide in their educational division.

A frequent keynote speaker at educational conferences, "Miss Jackie" is a sure bet to be a presenter at any national meeting she can fit into her busy schedule. She presents dozens of concerts annually for children and their parents.

**For a FREE Miss Jackie Music Company catalog,
please write:**
Miss Jackie Music Co.
10001 El Monte, Department BG
Overland Park, KS 66207
(913) 381-3672